(5OO plus Book List)

Africans In History

Register for and on behalf of:

Ma'arifa Development Organisation

https://www.maarifado.com

Authors: PTR LMDumizulu & Prince A.B. Udo Ibiono.

INTRODUCTION...

We are extremely thrilled. You have taken a massive step to acquire your lethal weapons. Your incredible list of over *500 books,* researched and written by Top world re-known Thinkers is now all Yours. Since they say hide it in books, we say *find it in books!*

YOU Are conscious Of Our True BaNtu- (Afrikan/Negroid) Identity which

allows YOU to apply all original spiritual and physical principles (Laws) as

Your Winners take all Formula. **ONCE you start reading some thought-**

provoking books here and there you become aware that your ancestors

had home libraries. **You immediately want yours too. They were fond of**

books some were buried holding their favorite copies.

You have made the best choice because listed here, are books you

would die for. Your Self-esteem, Confidence and Mental Focus will

become formidable. These Books are Your greatest weapon, a

solid, indestructible connection to Your rich and Great Ancestry.

Knowledge is one of the countless tools You must have. **BUT It**

is Applied Knowledge which Is a differential factor to those who

make it in Life. In saying this You have stepped Up to Unleash

Your Greatness. Now this will be guaranteed. Order Your copies

and build that ancestral library.

Once again Let This Enhance YOUR Knowledge Big time.

To the Researchers and Authors Thank You!

Applied KNOWLEDGE Is POWER!

Some of the Authors include but are not limited to;

Dr. John Henrik Clarke

Dr. Ben Yusuf Jochannan

Indus Khamit-Kush

Dr Joy DeGruy

Ra Un Nefer Amen (SPECIAL BOOKS ON MA'AT)

Dr George G. M. James

Ivan Van Sertima

Cheikh Anta Diop

Dr Theophile Obenga

Chancellor Williams and W. E. B. Du Bois

Dr Acholonu Catherine

John G. Jackson

Prince Hall Freemasonry

The Honorable Marcus Garvey

J. A. Rogers

Supreme Understanding Allah

Dr Walter Williams

Aqiyl Aniys

John Alembillah Azumah

Maulana Karenga

Jacob Carruthers

Willie Lynch

Dr. Claud Anderson

Anthony T. Browder

Snowden Jr., Frank M.

Stanley Lane-Poole

Carter Goodwin Woodson

Dr Frances Cress Welsing

E. A. Wallis Budge

Dr Molefi Kete Asante

Dr Llaila Afrika

Dr Muata Ashby.

Runoko Rashidi

Wim van den Dungen

Moustafa Gadalla

Gabriel A. Oyibo

Gerald Massey

PTR LMDumizulu

Titles on Hot Topics…

Captivating History Books by various authors

OLDEST SURVIVING BOOKS, PAPYRUS AND HIEROGLYPHICS

African Entrepreneurial Books.

Modern Day African Logic Book

Learning and mastering hieroglyphics

Your Game Changing Book List

Books: By Dr. John Henrik Clarke

1. American Negro Short Stories By: John Henrik Clarke
2. African People in World History (Black Classic Press Contemporary Lecture) (Black Classic Press Contemporary Lecture) (Black Classic Press Contemporary Lecture) By: John Henrik Clarke
3. Christopher Columbus and the Afrikan Holocaust: Slavery and the Rise of European Capitalism By: John Henrik Clarke
4. My Life in Search of Africa by: John Henrik Clarke
5. Africans at the Crossroad: Notes on an African World Revolution By: John Henrik Clarke
6. Rebellion in Rhyme By: John Henrik Clarke
7. African American Literature: Globe Multicultural Literature Collection By: John Henrik Clarke
8. Who Betrayed the African World Revolution? And Other Speeches By: John Henrik Clarke
9. The Early Years By: John Henrik Clarke
10. Cheikh Anta Diop And the New Light on African History by John Henrik Clarke
11. New Dimensions in African History: The London Lectures of Dr. Yosef Ben-Jochannan and Dr. John Henrik Clarke

12. Iceman Inheritance: Prehistoric Sources of Western Man's Racism, Sexism and Aggression Jun 1, 1991 by Michael Bradley, John Henrik Clarke

13. Malcolm X: The Man and His Times Oct 1, 1969: By John Henrik Clarke

Books by Dr. Ben Yusuf Jochannan

14. Africa; Lands, Peoples, And Cultures of The World By: Yosef A.A. Ben-Jochannan

15. Africa: Mother of Western Civilization (African-American Heritage Series) By: Yosef A.A. Ben-Jochannan

16. Africa; Lands, Peoples, And Cultures of The World by Yosef A.A. Ben-Jochannan

17. Africa: Mother of Western Civilization (African-American Heritage Series)

18. African Origins of the Major "Western Religions" by Yosef A.A. Ben-Jochannan

19. From Afrikan Captives to Insane Slaves: The Need for Afrikan History in Solving the "Black" Mental Health Crisis in "America" and the World by Yosef A.A. Ben-Jochannan

20. The Need for a Black Bible by Yosef A.A. Ben-Jochannan

21. Chronology of the Bible by Yosef A.A. Ben-Jochannan

Indus Khamit-Kush

Ra Un Nefer Amen (SPECIAL BOOKS ON MA'AT)

31. **Metu Neter, Vol. 1: The Great Oracle of Tehuti and the Egyptian System of Spiritual Cultivation Paperback – by Ra Un Nefer Amen (Author)**

32. **Maat the 11 laws of God: By Ra Un Nefer Amen**

33. **Metu Neter Vol. 2: Anuk Ausar, The Kamitic Initiation System: By Ra Un Nefer Amen**

34. **Metu Neter Vol.3 the key to miracles: By Ra Un Nefer Amen**

35. **Nuk Au Neter (I am a Divine Being): The Kamitic Holy Scriptures: By Ra Un Nefer Amen**

36. **Tree of Life Meditation System (T.O.L.M.) :By Ra Un Nefer Amen**

37. **Men Ab: Kamitic Behavioral Transcendence Meditation: By Ra Un Nefer Amen**

38. **An Afrocentric Guide to a Spiritual Union: By Ra Un Nefer Amen**

39. **Healing the Errors of Living: By Ra Un Nefer Amen**

George G. M. James

Ivan Van Sertima

By Cheikh Anta Diop

John G. Jackson

Chancellor Williams and W. E. B. Du Bois

73. Destruction of Black Civilization: Great Issues of a Race from 4500 B.C. to 2000 A.D.: By Chancellor Williams, Joseph Kent, et al.

74. The Rebirth of African Civilization: By Chancellor Williams

75. From Babylon to Timbuktu: A History of the Ancient Black Races Including the Black Hebrews: By Rudolph R Windsor and El Hagahn

76. By W. E. B. Du Bois -The Souls of Black Folk (Dover Thrift Editions):

77. When The World Was Black: The Untold Story of the World's First Civilizations, Part 2 - Ancient Civilizations (Science of Self): By Supreme Understanding

78. The Souls of Black Folk (Enriched Classics) By: Dubois, W.E.B.

79. Black Reconstruction By: Dubois, W.E.B.

80. The Crisis By: Dubois, W.E.B.

81. Dark water: Voices from within the Veil: By W. E. B. Du Bois, Bernard K. Addison, et al

82. The Negro: By W.E.B. Du Bois

83. The Titan: By W.E.B. Du Bois

84. **W.E.B. Du Bois: An Encyclopedia By Gerald Horne; Mary Young**

85. **The Open Sore of a Continent: A Personal Narrative of the Nigerian Crisis (W.E.B. Du Bois Institute):** By Wole Soyinka

Prince Hall Freemasonry

86. **Prince Hall Freemasonry: The Secret Within Paperback: By Warrior Hawk**

87. **Ebros Masonic Symbol Freemasonry Square and Compasses Ritual Morality Hinged Book Box 5.75"Long Small Jewelry Box Container**

88. **Duncan's Ritual of Freemasonry Paperback – April 12, 1976: By Malcolm C. Duncan**

89. **101 Secrets of the Freemasons: The Truth Behind the World's Most Mysterious Society Hardcover –: By Barb Karg and John K Young**

90. **Letters to My Teacher: Tributes to the People Who Have Made a Difference: By Barb Karg and Rick Sutherland**

91. **Letters To My Mother: Tributes To The Women Who Give Us Life--And Love By Barb Karg and Rick Sutherland**

92. **The History Detectives Explore Lincoln's Letter, Parker's Sax, and Mark Twain's Watch: And Many More Mysteries of America's Past: By Barb Karg**

93. Secret America: The Hidden Symbols, Codes and Mysteries of the United States: By Barb Karg

94. The Everything Freemasons Book: Unlock the Secrets of This Ancient And Mysterious Society! (Everything (History & Travel)):By John K. Young and Barb Karg

95. The 66 Laws of the Illuminati: Secrets of Success: By The House of Illuminati and LLC Creative Works Holdings

96. Solomon's Builders: Freemasons, Founding Fathers and the Secrets of Washington D.C.: By Christopher Hodapp

97. The Everything Filmmaking Book: From Script to Premiere -a Complete Guide to Putting Your Vision on the Screen: By Barb Karg, Rick Sutherland, et al.

98. The World's Stupidest Politicians: By Barb Karg and Rick Sutherland

99. The World's Stupidest Men: By Barb Karg and Rick Sutherland

100. Sacred Sites of the Knights Templar: The Ancient Secrets Hidden in Stonehenge, Rennesle-Chateau, and Santiago de Compostela: The Ancient Secrets Hidden and Santiago De Compostela By John K Young

101. **Duncan's Masonic Ritual and Monitor Or a Guide to the Three Symbolic Degrees of the Ancient York Rite, Mark Master, Past**

102. **Master, Most Excellent Master and the Royal Arch: By Malcolm C. Duncan**

103. **The Royal Arch Or Seventh Degree Illustrated: By Malcolm C. Duncan**

The Honorable Marcus Garvey

104. **Selected Writings and Speeches of Marcus Garvey (Dover Thrift Editions): By Marcus Garvey and Bob Blaisdell**

105. **Philosophy and Opinions of Marcus Garvey [Volumes I & II in One Volume]: By Marcus Garvey and Amy Jacques Garvey**

106. **Message to the People: By Marcus Garvey**

107. **Negro with a Hat: The Rise and Fall of Marcus Garvey: By Colin Grant**

108. **The Philosophy and Opinions of Marcus Garvey, Or, Africa for the Africans (The New Marcus Garvey Library, No. 9): By Marcus Garvey and Amy Jacques Garvey**

109. **Emancipated from Mental Slavery: Selected Sayings of Marcus Garvey: By Nnamdi Azikiwe**

110. **The Tragedy of White Justice: By Marcus Garvey**

111. Message to the People: The Course of African Philosophy (On Grenada) by Marcus Garvey (1986-09-01) By Marcus Garvey

112. The Gospel According to Marcus Garvey: His Philosophies & Opinions about Christ: By Hon Marcus Mosiah Garvey, Mr Brian Lee Edwards, et al.

113. They Had a Dream: The Civil Rights Struggle from Frederick Douglass to Marcus Garvey to Martin Luther King and Malcolm X: By Jules Archer, Roscoe Orman, et al.

114. Marcus Garvey Life and Lessons: A Centennial Companion to the Marcus Garvey and Universal Negro Improvement Association Papers: By Marcus Garvey, Robert Abraham Hill, et al.

J. A. Rogers

100 Amazing Facts About the Negro with Complete Proof: A Short Cut to The World History of The Negro Paperback – June 15, 1980: By J. A. Rogers

115. **Nature Knows No Color-Line: Research Into the Negro Ancestry in the White Race May 24, 2018: By J Rogers**

116. **Your History: From Beginning of Time to the Present Jan By J Rogers**

117. **Africa's Gift to America: The Afro-American in the Making and Saving of the United States Sep 15, 2014: By J. A. Rogers**

118. **World's Great Men of Color, Volume I May 17, 2011: By J.A. Rogers, John Henrik Clarke**

119. **World's Great Men of Color, Volume II Jul 6, 2010: By J.A. Rogers, John Henrik Clarke**

120. **Sex and Race: A History of White, Negro, and Indian Miscegenation in the Two Americas, Vol. 2: The New World By J.A. Rogers**

Supreme Understanding Allah

Knowledge of Self: A Collection of Wisdom on the Science of Everything in Life: By C'BS Alife Allah, Supreme Understanding Allah, Sunez Allah, Lord Jamar Kindle Edition

128. **The Science of Self: By Dr. Supreme Understanding**

129. **How to Hustle and Win: A Survival Guide for the Ghetto By Dr. Supreme Understanding**

130. **When the World was Black Part One: Prehistoric Cultures Dr. Supreme Understanding**

131. **Black God: By Dr. Supreme Understanding**

132. **When The World Was Black: The Untold Story of the World's First Civilizations, Part 2 - Ancient Civilizations (Science of Self): By Supreme Understanding**

133. **How to Hustle and Win, Part 2: Rap, Race, and Revolution By Supreme Understanding**

134. **The Hood Health Handbook: A Practical Guide to Health and Wellness in the Urban Community (Volume One) By Supreme Understanding**

135. **365 Days of Real Black History: Little-known Facts of the Global Black Experience from Prehistory to the Present By Supreme Understanding**

136. **Rap, Race and Revolution: Solutions for Our Struggle By Supreme Understanding**

Aqiyl Aniys

137. **Alkaline Herbal Medicine: Reverse Disease And Heal The Electric Body Sep 18, 2016: By Aqiyl Aniys**

138. **Alkaline Plant Based Diet: Reversing Disease and Saving the Planet with an Alkaline Plant Based Diet, The God-Awakening Diet By: Aqiyl Aniys**

139. **Faith and Justice eat an Alkaline Plant Based Diet By: Aqiyl Aniys**

140. **The Autobiography of Emperor Haile Sellassie I: King of Kings of All Ethiopia and Lord of All Lords (My Life and Ethiopia's Progress) (My Life... ... (My Life and Ethiopia's Progress (Paperback)) Paperback – March 1, 1999 by Haile I. Sellassie**

141. **[THE AUTOBIOGRAPHY OF EMPEROR HAILE SELLASSIE I: KING OF ALL KINGS AND LORD OF ALL LORDS; MY LIFE AND ETHIOPIA'S PROGRESS 1892-1937 (MASS MARKET) (MY LIFE AND ETHIOPIA'S PROGRESS (PAPERBACK) #2)] By Sellassie, Haile (Author) 1999 [Paperback] by Haile Sellassie**

142. **The Coronation of H.I.M. Emperor Haile Sellassie 1: Addis, 1930**

143. **My Life and Ethiopia's Progress: The Autobiography of Emperor Haile Sellassie I (Volume 1) (My Life and Ethiopia's Progress) (My Life and Ethiopia's Progress) by Haile I. Selassie (1999) Paperback**

144. **The Autobiography of Emperor Haile Sellassie I: King of All Kings and Lord of All Lords; My Life and Ethiopia's Progress 1892-1937 * *Author: Haile Sellassie**

145. **Haile Selassie I was Ethiopia's 225th and last emperor, serving from 1930 until his overthrow by the Marxist dictator Mengistu Haile Mariam in 1974. The longtime ruler traced his line back to Menelik I, who was credited with being the child of King Solomon and the Queen of Sheba.**

146. **The Legacy of ARAB-ISLAM IN AFRICA By**: John Alembillah Azumah

147. **Ma'at, The Moral Ideal In Ancient Egypt By: Maulana Karenga A Study In Classical African Ethics**

157. Charles H. Wesley: The Intellectual Tradition of a Black Historian (Studies in African American History and Culture):

158. By James L. Conyers Jr.

159. From the Browder File Vol II: Survival Strategies for Africans in America: 13 Steps to Freedom: By Anthony T. Browder

160. Nile Valley Contributions to Civilization (Exploding the Myths): By Anthony T. Browder

161. Nile Valley Contributions to Civilization Workbook: By Anthony T. Browder

Stanley Lane-Poole

162. The Story of the Moors After Spain: By Stanley Lane-poole

163. The Story of the Moors in Spain Paperback: By Stanley Lane-Poole

164. The Moors in Spain (Illustrated): By Stanley Lane-Poole

165. Saladin and the Fall of the Kingdom of Jerusalem: By Stanley Lane-Poole

166. The Story of the Barbary Corsairs: By Stanley Lane-Poole, J. D. Jerrold (James Douglas Jerrold)

167. The story of Turkey: By Stanley Lane-Poole

168. Rulers Of India: Aurangzeb, Emperor of Hindustan, 1618-1707: By Stanley Lane-Poole

169. A history of Egypt in the Middle Ages: By Stanley Lane-Poole

170. **The Speeches & Table-talk of the Prophet Mohammad; Chosen and Translated, With Introd. and Notes by Stanley Lane-Poole: By Lane-Poole, Stanley**

171. **Saladin: All-Powerful Sultan and the Uniter of Islam: By Stanley Lane-Poole**

172. **The Mohammadan Dynasties, Chronological and Genealogical Tables with Historical Introductions: By Stanley Lane-Poole**

173. **The Art of the Saracens in Egypt (1886): By Stanley Lane Poole**

174. **Studies in a Mosque: By Stanley Lane-Poole**

Carter Goodwin Woodson

175. **The Mis-Education of the Negro: By Carter Goodwin Woodson, Anthony Stewart, The Anthony Report**

176. **The Miseducation of the Negro: By Carter Godwin Woodson**

177. **The History of the Negro Church: By Carter Godwin Woodson**

178. **The Negro in Our History: By Carter Godwin Woodson**

179. **The Education of the Negro Prior to 1861 A History of the Education of the Colored People of the United States from the Beginning of Slavery to the Civil War: By Carter Godwin Woodson**

180. **The Mis-Education of the Negro (Includes Study Guide) [Annotated]:By Carter Godwin Woodson**

181. **African Myths and Folk Tales (Dover Children's Thrift Classics) :By Carter Godwin Woodson**

182. **Free Negro Owners of Slaves in the United States in 1830: Together with Absentee Ownership of Slaves in the United States in 1830: By Carter G. Woodson**

183. **AFRICAN HEROES AND HEROINES (The Woodson Series): By Carter Goodwin Woodson, Charles H. Wesley, Daryl Michael Scott**

184. **The mind of the Negro as reflected in letters written during the crisis, 1800-1860: By Carter Godwin Woodson**

Dr Theophile Obenga

193. **Ancient Egypt and Black Africa First Edition: by Theophile Obenga**
194. **African Philosophy: The Pharaonic Period: 2780 - 330 BC -By Theophile Obenga**
195. **African Philosophy During the Period of the Pharaohs 2780-330 BCE: By Theophile Obenga**
196.

Frances Cress Welsing

197. **The Isis Papers: The Keys to the Colors: By Dr. Frances Cress Welsing**
198. **Black Child Journal: Racism and the Black Child (Tribute to Dr. Frances Cress Welsing)**
199. **The Cress Theory of Color Confrontation and Racism (White Supremacy) (A Psycho-Genetic Theory and World Outlook): By Frances C Welsing - The Isis (Yssis) Papers (11.1.1991)**
200. **Race Code War: The Power of Words, Images, and Symbols on the Black Psych: By Khari Enaharo**

E. A. Wallis Budge:

201. The Ancient Egyptian Book of the Dead: Prayers, Incantations, and Other Texts from the Book of the Dead By E. A. Wallis Budge

202. The Egyptian Book of the Dead: The Papyrus of Ani in the British Museum: By E. A. Wallis Budge

203. The Book Of The Dead: By E. A. Wallis Budge – Illustrated: By E. A. Wallis Budge

204. The Book of the Dead: Hieroglyphic Transcript and Translation into English of the Papyrus of Ani by Sir E a Wallis Budge (1995-12-31)

205. Theban Recension of the Book of the Dead: The Chapters of Coming Forth by Day: By E.A. Wallis Budge

206. The Egyptian Book of the Dead (Paperback)--by E. A. Wallis Budge [1967 Edition]: By E. A. Wallis Budge

207. The Egyptian Book of the Dead: The Papyrus of Ani in the British Museum: By E.A. Wallis Budge, Chris Matthews, et al.

208. Egyptian Book of the Dead, The: Papyrus of Ani (The Great Awakening): By Budge and E. A. Wallis

209. The Egyptian Book of the Dead: By Anonymous and E.A. Wallis Budge

210. Hieroglyphic Vocabulary to the Book of the Dead (Egypt) by E. A. Wallis Budge (2011-11-30)

211. Legends of the Gods: The Egyptian Texts, edited with Translations: By Sir E. A. Wallis Budge

212. Hieroglyphic vocabulary to the Theban recession of the Book of the dead, With an index to all the English equivalents of the Egyptian words, by E.A. Wallis Budge (Books on Egypt and Chaldea) by E. A. Wallis Budge

213. The Egyptian Book of the Dead by E. A. Wallis Budge (2005-07-16)

214. [The Egyptian Book of the Dead (Egypt) (English, Egyptian) By Budge, E A Wallis (Author) Paperback 1967]: By E A Wallis Budge

215. The Book of the Dead: From the Tomb of Ani (Classic Book Series): By E.A. Wallis Budge

216. Osiris and the Egyptian Resurrection, Vol. 1 & 2: By E. A. Wallis Budge

217. Daily Life of the Ancient Egyptians, 2nd Edition: By Bob M. Brier and Hoyt Hobbs

218. Daily Life of the Ancient Egyptians: By Bob Brier and Hoyt Hobbs

Dr Molefi Kete Asante

219. The Book of African Names: By Molefi Kete Asante
220. The Egyptian Philosophers: Ancient African Voices from Imhotep to Akhenaten: By Molefi Kete Asante
221. Encyclopedia of African Religion: By Molefi Kete Asante and Ama Mazama
222. Encyclopedia of Black Studies: By Molefi Kete Asante and Mambo Ama Mazama
223. 100 Greatest African Americans: A Biographical Encyclopedia by Asante, Molefi Kete (2003)
224. Introduction to African Religion: By Molefi Kete and Emeka Nwadiora
225. ARAB RACISM IN KUSH: The Adventures and Opinions of Bol Gai Deng (Ainu Edition) :By Bol Gai Deng and Molefi Kete Asante
226. Revolutionary Pedagogy: By Molefi Kete Asante
227. The History of Africa: By Molefi Kete Asante
228. The Book of African Names: By Molefi Kete Asante
229. The Egyptian Philosophers: Ancient African Voices from Imhotep to Akhenaten: By Molefi Kete Asante

Slave Revivalists Who created their World.

240. **The Immortal Life of Henrietta Lacks Unabridged edition by Skloot, Rebecca (2010) Hardcover: By Rebecca Skloot**

The Immortal Life of Henrietta Lacks

African-American History Books, Books, Non-Black author, her name was Henrietta Lacks, but scientists know her as HeLa. She was a poor black tobacco farmer whose cells—taken without her knowledge in 1951—became one of the most important tools in medicine, vital and were the first immortal human cell line—the cells reproduce infinitely in a lab. For research.

241. **Horace King: From Slave, to Master Builder and Legislator (An African American Experience Project): By J. David Dameron**

Self-Taught Engineer

Horace King: Bridges to Freedom by Faye Gibbons is a compelling biography of nineteenth-century master bridge builder Horace King. A former enslaved man who worked to buy his own freedom, King was remarkable am...

242. **Bridging Deep South Rivers: The Life and Legend of Horace King: By John S. Lupold and Thomas L. French Jr.**

Bridging Deep South Rivers: The Life and Legend of Horace King. Biography/Memoir, Books. Horace King (1807-1885) built covered bridges over every large river in Georgia, Alabama, and eastern Mississippi.

That King, who began life as an enslaved man in Cheraw, South Carolina, received no formal trail

243. **Pioneers Of The Black Atlantic: Five Slave Narratives, 1772-1815: By Henry Louis Gates.**
Captivity Narrative

In the eighteenth century, a small group of Black men met the challenge of the Enlightenment by mastering the arts and sciences and writing themselves into history. The battle lines were clear—literacy stood ...

244. **Chronicles of Mankind: A New World: By C.A. Morrison and Cindy**

Wim van den Dungen. Belgium (Scholar and Philosopher)

Review his books

245. **ANCIENT EGYPTIAN READINGS: By Wim van den Dungen**
246. **The Egyptian Gentleman (The Maxims of Good Discourse): By Wim van den Dungen**
247. **On Seven Ways of Holy Love: By Wim Van Den Dungen**
248. **Ten Ox-Herding Images: By Wim van den Dungen**
249. **The Books of Enoch: Complete edition: Including (1) The Ethiopian Book of Enoch, (2) The Slavonic Secrets and (3) The Hebrew Book of Enoch: By Paul C. Schneider's and Robert H. Charles**

260. **The Holy Koran of the Moorish Science Temple of America:**
By Drew Ali

261. **The Holy Koran of the Moorish Science Temple of America:**
By Noble Drew Ali and C. S. Moore

262. **Shaikh Daoud Vs. W.D. Fard:** By Dr. Malachi Z. York

263. **Flavius Josephus, William Whiston, et al. Jews scholar,**
Historian and writer

264. **The Complete Works of Josephus: By Flavius Josephus,**
William Whiston, et al.

265. **The Complete Works of Flavius Josephus - Legendary Jewish**
Historian and His Chronicle of Ancient History: By translation
by William Whiston

266. **The Works of Flavius Josephus [4 Vols]: By Flavius Josephus**
and William Whiston

267. **Adam's Rib, Creation & The Human Body: By Carl Wieland**

268. **The Genesis Account: A theological, historical, and scientific**
commentary on Genesis 1-11: By Jonathan Sarfati

269. **The Creation Answers Book: By David Catchpoole , Jonathan**
Sarfati , et al.

270. **The Jesus Myth: By G. A. Wells**

271. **Christianity's Debt to Judaism: Why Not Acknowledge it? By**
John Haynes Holmes

272. Ceremonies, rites and traditions of the Jews: interspersed with gleanings from the Jerusalem and Babylonian Talmud, and the

273. Targums, Mishna, Gemara, ... published, also a copious selections ... [183-] :By Hyam Isaacs

274. A Spiritual and Ethical Compendium to the Torah and Talmud: By Arthur Segal and Frank Dunne Jr.

275. A History of the Early Korean Kingdom of Paekche's, together with an annotated translation of <i>The Paekche Annals</i> of the <i>Samguk sagi</i> (Harvard East Asian Monographs): By Jonathan W. Best

Runoko Rashidi

276. **My Global Journeys in Search of the African Presence - Runoko Rashidi: By Runoko Rashidi**

277. **Black Star: the African Presence in Early Europe: By Runoko Rashidi**

278. **African Star Over Asia: The Black Presence in the East: By Runoko Rashidi**

279. **Afrikan Theology Cosmogony & Philosophy: By Edow Butweiku I and Runoko Rashidi**

280. **When We Ruled: The Ancient and Mediaeval History of Black Civilizations: By Robin Walker.**

281. **The Wisdom of Ben-Sira: (Ecclesiasticus) (Classic Reprint): By W. O. E. Oesterley**

282. **The Wisdom of Ben-Sira (Ecclesiasticus): By Bible.**

283. **Wisdom Books: Job, Psalms, Proverbs, Ecclesiastes, Song of Songs, Wisdom, Sirach (Ben Sira) (Liguori Catholic Bible Study): By William Anderson**

284. **The Search for the Christian Doctrine of God: The Arian Controversy, 318-381: By R. P. C. Hanson A Dissertation Concerning the Eternal Sonship Of Christ and The Arian Controversy: By Dr. John Gill D.D., Henry Melville Gwatkins, et al.**

285. The true authorship of the New Testament: By Abelard Reuchlin

286. The True Authorship of the New Testament: By ARIUS CALPURNIUS PISO PEN NAME FALVIUS JOSEPHUS

287. The Apocalypse Deception: The Book of Revelation is not what it claims to be: By Fred Harding

288. Did Jesus Live 100 B.C.? : By G. R. S. Mead

289. Did Jesus Live 100 B.C.? An Inquiry into The Talmud Jesus Stories, The Toldoth Jeschu, And Some Curious Statements Of Epiphanius - Being A Contribution To The Study Of Christian Origins: By G.R.S. Mead B.A.

290. Chaminuka - Prophet of Zimbabwe: By Solomon T. Mutswairo

291. The case of African prophecy-The unknown phenomenon that need to be known.: Prophecy - Unlocking the mysteries: By Mr Michael P M Mhlanga, Mr Dornald M Mhlanga, et al.

292. The Crisis of the 17th Century (Religion, the Reformation, and Social Change):By Hugh Trevor-Roper

293. The Rise Of Christian Europe: History Of European Civilization Library General Editor Geoffrey Barraclough: By Hugh Trevor-Roper

294. The Ishango Bone: By Paul Hastings Wilson

295. **Africa and Mathematics: From Colonial Findings Back to the Ishango Rods (Mathematics, Culture, and the Arts) :By Dirk Huylebrouck**

296. **African Mathematics: From Bones to Computers: By Abdul Karim Bangura**

297. **Kipsigis (Heritage Library of African Peoples):By Abdul Karim Bangura**

298. **Managing Conflicts in Africa's Democratic Transitions: By Akanmu G. Adebayo, Oluwakemi Abiodun Adesina, et al.**

299. **The Universal Book of Mathematics: From Abracadabra to Zeno's Paradoxes: By David Darling**

300. **Scale: The Universal Laws of Growth, Innovation, Sustainability, and the Pace of Life, in Organisms, Cities, Economies, and Companies: By Geoffrey West, Bruce Mann, et al.**

301. **The World's Great Speeches: 292 Speeches from Pericles to Mandela (Fourth Enlarged Edition) (Dover): By Lewis Copeland, Lawrence W. Lamm, et al.**

302. **The World's Great Speeches: Fourth Enlarged (1999) edition: By Lewis Copeland, Lawrence W. Lamm, et al.**

303. **The Greatest Speech, Ever: By James L. Cotton Jr.**

304. **Handbook of African Medicinal Plants: By Maurice M. Iwu**

305. New Age Bible of Mother Africa (Vol.2): Black Consciousness, Ancient Alien Gods, Metaphysics, Kemetic Spirituality & African Origins of Civilization (Volume 2): By T Lindsey-Billingsley

306. New Age Bible of Mother Africa: Genetic Engineering, Human Phylogeny, Lost Civilizations, Ancient Knowledge, The Metu Neter & the Anunnaki Gods of Nibiru: By T Lindsey-Bilingsley

307. Conversations with Ogotemmeli: An Introduction to Dogon Religious Ideas: By Marcel Griaule and Germaine Dieterlen

308. Maa Aankh: The Kamitic Shaman Way of Working the Superconscious Mind to Improve Memory, Solve Problems

309. Intuitively and Spiritually Grow Through the Power of the Spirits: By Derric Moore

310. New Age Bible of Mother Africa: Genetic Engineering, Human Phylogeny, Lost Civilizations, Ancient Knowledge, The Metu Neter & the Anunnaki Gods of Nibiru

311. Nuk Au Neter (I am a Divine Being): The Kamitic Holy Scriptures: By Ra Un Nefer Amen

312. Men Ab: Kamitic Behavioral Transcendence Meditation: By Ra Un Nefer Amen

313. Healing Is in the Spirit (Book and Cd): By Ra Un Nefer Amen

314. UAAB vol 1: Heal & Enhance Your Brain with Kamitic Meditation: By Ra Un Nefer Amen (2013-08-02): By Ra Un Nefer Amen

Captivating History

360. **Early Civilizations of the Old World: The Formative Histories of Egypt, The Levant, Mesopotamia, India and China: By Charles Keith Maisels**

361. **The Archaeology of Politics and Power: Where, When and Why the First States Formed by Charles Keith Maisels: By Charles Keith Maisels**

362. **The emergence of civilization: From hunting and gathering to agriculture, cities, and the state in the Near East: By Charles Keith Maisels**

363. **Animal Totems and Spirit Guides: The Wisdom of Owl (Volume 1) Paperback By: Jordana Van**

364. **Animal Totems and Spirit Guides: The Wisdom of Snake By: Jordana Van**

365. **Animal Totems and the Gemstone Kingdom: Spiritual Connections of Crystal Vibrations and Animal Medicine Paperback: By Margaret Ann Lembo**

366. **Totem Animals, Plain & Simple: By: Celia M Gunn**

367. **Simply® Totem Animals (Simply® Series) By: Celia M. Gunn, Zambezi Publishing**

368. **Nature Spirituality From the Ground Up: Connect with Totems in Your Ecosystem: By Lupa**

369. New Paths to Animal Totems: Three Alternative Approaches to Creating Your Own Totemism By: Lupa

370. New Paths to Animal Totems: Three Alternative Approaches to Creating Your Own Totemism Paperback By: Lupa

Dr Acholonu Catherine

371. Acholonu Catherine, et. al. The Gram Code of African Adam – Reconstructing 450,000 Years of Africa's Lost Civilizations

372. Acholonu, Catherine et.al.; They Lived Before Adam: Prehistoric Origins of the Igbo, The Never Been Ruled

373. Acholonu, Catherine et.al.; The Lost Testament of the Ancestors of Adam: Unearthing Heliopolis/Igbo Ukwu – The Celestial City of the Gods of Egypt and Dravidian India (2010).

374. Acholonu Catherine; "Igbo – A Former Global Lingua Franca and The Mother of Semitic Languages", 2011 ISA Conference, Howard University, Washington DC.

375. Acholonu, Catherine; "Igbo The Origin of Languages and Civilizations", 2010 World Igbo Congress, Philadelphia, USA

376. Hieroglyphics of Horapollo Nilous: By Horapollo

377. The Hieroglyphics of Horapollo Nilous: Hieroglyphic Semantics in Late Antiquity (Issues in Ancient Philosophy): By Mark Wildish

378. By Amen Maat-Ra The Roman Illusion Volume One: Explores the African origins of Christianity (Volume 1) (2nd Second Edition) [Paperback]

379. The Roman Illusion Volume One: Explores the African origins of Christianity (Volume 1): By Amen Maat-Ra

380. Outlines of the History of Greek Philosophy: By Edward, Zeller,

381. Outlines of the History of Greek Philosophy: By Eduard Zeller

382. A Student's History of Philosophy: -1916: By Arthur Kenyon Rogers

383. A Student's History of Philosophy: -1913: By Arthur Kenyon Rogers

384. A Student's History of Philosophy Arthur Kenyon Rogers Hardcover Third Edition 1933

385. The History Book: Big Ideas Simply Explained: By DK

386. Melanin: What makes Black People Black Paperback – October 9, 2009: By Llaila Afrika

387. Post Traumatic Slave Syndrome, Revised Edition: America's Legacy of Enduring Injury and Healing: By Dr Joy DeGruy

388. Greatness Is in Our DNA: From Being Worshipped Like Gods to Victims of Post Traumatic Slave Syndrome, Volume III: By Dr. Rufus O. Jimerson

389. Black psychology: By Reginald Lanier Jones

390. Black Psychology, Fourth Edition: By Reginald Lanier Jones

391. Emancipated from Mental Slavery: By Marcus Garvey and Nnamdi Azikiwe

392. Born in Captivity: Psychopathology as a Legacy of Slavery: By Rick Wallace

393. 12 MILLION BLACK VOICES By Richard Wright

394. Invisible Life by E. Lynn Harris

African Entrepreneurial Books

395. Black Titan: A.G. Gaston and the Making of a Black American Millionaire: By Carol Jenkins and Elizabeth Gardner Hines

396. Black Labor, White Wealth: The Search for Power and Economic Justice: By Claud Anderson

397. Why Should White Guys Have All the Fun? How Reginald Lewis Created a Billion-Dollar Business Empire: By Reginald F. Lewis and Blair S. Walker

398. Black Titan: A.G. Gaston and the Making of a Black American Millionaire: By Carol Jenkins and Elizabeth Gardner Hines

399. Outliers: The Story of Success: By Malcolm Gladwell

400. Life Ahead: On Learning and the Search for Meaning: By J. Krishnamurti

401. The Shining Ones: The World's Most Powerful Secret Society Revealed:By Philip Gardiner and Gary Osborn

402. Physicians of the Soul: The Psychologies of the World's Greatest Spiritual Leaders: By Robert May

403. The Kingdom of the Cults: An Analysis of the Major Cult Systems in The Present by Walter R. Martin

404. **Capitalism and Slavery by Eric Williams**

405. **Economic Facts and Fallacies, 2nd edition by Thomas Sowell**

406. **More Liberty Means Less Government: Our Founders Knew This Well (Hoover Institution Press Publication) by Walter E. Williams**

407. **The Historical Origin of Islam by Walter Williams**

408. **Liberty Versus the Tyranny of Socialism: Controversial Essays by Walter E. Williams**

Moustafa Gadalla

409. Historical Deception: The Untold Story of Ancient Egypt - Second Edition: by Moustafa Gadalla

410. The Musical Aspects of the Ancient Egyptian Vocalic Language: by Moustafa Gadalla

411. Egyptian Alphabetical Letters of Creation Cycle:by Moustafa Gadalla

412. The Untainted Egyptian Origin: Why Ancient Egypt Matters: by Moustafa Gadalla

413. Exiled Egyptians: The Heart of Africa: by Moustafa Gadalla

414. Isis The Divine Female: By Moustafa Gadalla

415. Egyptian Alphabetical Letters of Creation Cycle: by Moustafa Gadalla

416. The Temple of Man by Schwaller de Lubicz, R. A.

417. Sacred Science: The King of Pharaonic Theocracy by Schwaller de Lubicz, R. A.

418. A Study of Numbers: A Guide to the Constant Creation of the Universe by Schwaller de Lubicz, R. A.

419. Esoterism and Symbol: by Schwaller de Lubicz, R. A.

420. Symbol and the Symbolic: Ancient Egypt, Science, and the Evolution of Consciousness: by Schwaller de Lubicz, R. A.

421. Al-Kemi: Hermetic, Occult, Political and Private Aspects of R. A. Schwaller De Lubicz (Inner Traditions/Lindisfarne Press uroboros series): by Andre Vandenbroeck

422. Her-Bak: Egyptian Initiate: by Isha S. Delubrcz

Gerald Massey

423. Man, In Search Of His Soul During Fifty Thousand Years And How He Found It by Gerald Massey

424. Egyptian Book of the Dead and the Ancient Mysteries of Amenta by Gerald Massey

425. That Old-Time Religion: The Story of Religious Foundations by Jordan Maxwell , Alan Snow, et al.

426. Lost Books of the Bible: The Great Rejected Texts by Joseph B. Lumpkin

427. The World's Oldest Alphabet: Hebrew As the Language of the Proto-consonantal Script: by Douglas Petrovich

428. Between the Lines of the Bible: A Modern Commentary on the 613 Commandments: by Herbert Samuel Goldstein

429. Israel In Britain: A Brief Statement Of The Evidences In Proof Of The Israelitish Origin Of The British Race: By Colonel Garnier and Mr Mark Guy Valerius Tyson

430. [(The Worship of the Dead or the Origin and Nature of Pagan Idolatry and Its Bearing Upon the Early History of Egypt and Babylonia)] [Author: Colonel J Garnier]

431. Mystery of the Ages: by Herbert W Armstrong

432. The Seven Laws of Success: by Herbert W. Armstrong

433. The United States and Britain in Prophecy: by Herbert W Armstrong

434. The Book of Revelation Unveiled at last!:by Herbert W. Armstrong

435. The Mystery of the Ages (Did You Ever Ask Yourself: "Who Am I? What Am I? Why Am I?" You Are a Mystery. The World About You Is a Mystery. Now, You Can Understand!):By Herbert W. Armstrong

436. Great Pyramid: Its Builder and Its Prophecy by Colonel Garnier (2003-04-07)

437. Frederick Douglass: Prophet of Freedom: By David W. Blight

438. The Complete Dead Sea Scrolls in English: Seventh Edition (Penguin Classics) 7th Edition: by Geza Vermes (Author)

439. Giovanni's Room: by James Baldwin

440. Go Tell It To The Mountain: by James Baldwin

441. The Fire Next Time: by James Baldwin

442. A History Of The Articles Of Religion. To Which Is Added A Series Of Documents, From A.d.1536 To A.d.1615by Charles Hardwick

443. The Generations Of Israel / The CBS Legacy Collection: by David Ben-Gurion, Edwin Herbert Viscount Samuel, et al.

444. The Mind of Arthur James Balfour: Selections From His Non-Political Writings, Speeches, and Addresses, 1878-1917, Including Special Sections on ... by Wilfrid M. Short (Classic Reprint):by Arthur James Balfour

445. Theism And Thought:by Arthur James Balfour

446. Theism and humanism, being the Gifford lectures delivered at the University of Glasgow, 1914:by Arthur James Balfour

447. Dred Scott v. Sandford: A Brief History with Documents (The Bedford Series in History and Culture):by Paul Finkelman

448. Dred Scott V. Sandford: Slavery and Freedom Before the American Civil War (Landmark Supreme Court Cases) by Amy Van Zee

449. Citizen or Slave: The Dred Scott Decision, 1857:by Matthew Pinsker, James G. Basker, et al.

459. **A Concise Dictionary of Egyptian Archaeology.: by Mary Brodrick**

460. The Oracle ((The Most Powerful Book in the World)): By Dr. Marcus Mandrake (Translator), Simon Lavoe (Illustrator)

461. **The Resurrectionist: The Lost Work of Dr. Spencer Black by E. B. Hudspeth**

Modern Day African Logic Book

462. **Introducing African Science: Systematic and Philosophical Approach (Studies in African Philosophy, Science, Logic and Mathematic):by Jonathan O. Chimakonam**

463. **Ezumezu: A System of Logic for African Philosophy and Studies: by Jonathan O. Chimakonam**

464. **Rules and Processes: The Cultural Logic of Dispute in an African Context: by John L. L. Comaroff and Simon Roberts**

465. **Listening for Africa: Freedom, Modernity, and the Logic of Black Music's African Origins:by David F. Garcia**

466. **White Logic, White Methods: Racism and Methodology: by Tukufu Zuberi and Eduardo Bonilla-Silva**

467. **Khnum-Ptah to Computer: The African Initialization of Computer Science: by Creation Energy, African**

468. **The Green Book: by Muammar Al Qaddafi**

Madrid Codex

Discovered in Spain in the 1860s, the Madrid Codex – also known as the Tro-Cortesianus Codex – is one of the only surviving books attributable to the pre-Columbian Maya culture of around 900–1521 AD.Most likely produced in Yucatán, the book is written in Yucatecan, a group of Mayan languages which includes Yucatec, Itza, Lacandon and Mopan.

469. **The Gutenberg Bible**

The Gutenberg Bible, also known as the 42-line Bible, is listed by the Guinness Book of World records as the world's oldest mechanically printed book – the first copies of which were printed in 1454-1455 AD.Printed by Johannes Gutenberg, in Mainz, Germany, it is considered to be oldest printed book using movable type in the West – though in China there were examples of book printing many centuries earlier, such as the Diamond Sutra.

470. **Celtic Psalter**

The Celtic Psalter is described as Scotland's Book of Kells. The pocket-sized book of Psalms is housed at the University of Edinburgh, where it went on public display in 2009 for the first time. The book is thought to be have been created in the 11th century AD, making it Scotland's oldest surviving book.

471. **Diamond Sutra**

A Buddhist holy text, the Diamond Sutra is considered to be the oldest surviving dated printed book in the world. Found in a walled-up cave in China along with other printed materials, the book is made up of Chinese characters printed on a scroll of grey printed paper, wrapped along a wooden pole

472. **Siddur, Jewish Prayer Book**

Discovered in 2013, the third major discovery this year, was a 'siddur' – a Jewish prayer book dated back to around 840 AD. The complete parchment, still in its original binding, is so old that it contains Babylonian vowel pointing – akin to the Old or Middle English for the English language.

473. **Book of Kells**

The Book of Kells is kept in the Trinity College Library in Dublin, Ireland, and is thought to have been created by Celtic monks around 800 AD. The book is an incredibly ornate illuminated manuscript Gospel book, written in Latin, containing the four Gospels of the New Testament.

474. St Cuthbert Gospel

Europe's oldest known surviving intact book is the St Cuthbert Gospel, bought by the British Library in 2012 for £9 million pounds as part of a fundraising campaign. The book was buried with St Cuthbert, an early British Christian leader, on the island of Lindisfarne off Northumberland, in around 698 AD.

475. Nag Hammadi Library

Considered to be some of the oldest surviving bound books – 13 leather bound papyrus codices were discovered in 1945 buried inside a sealed jar, by a local man in the town of Nag Hammadi in Upper Egypt.

476. Pyrgi Gold Tablets

Found in 1964 in the excavation of a sanctuary in ancient Pyrgi, Italy, the three gold plates date back to 500 Containing holes around the edges, scholars think they were once bound together. Two are written in Etruscan text, with one written in Phoenician – comprising of a dedication from King Thefarie Velianas to the Phoenician goddess Astarte. The plates are now displayed at the National Etruscan Museum in Rome, Italy.

477. Etruscan Gold Book

Thought to be the oldest multi-page book in the world, dating to about 660 BC, the Etruscan Gold Book was discovered 70 years ago whilst digging a canal off the Strouma river in Bulgaria. The book is made from 6 sheets of 24 carat gold, bound together with rings. The plates are written in Etruscan characters, and also depicted is a horse, horseman, a Siren, a lyre, and soldiers. The book was donated to Bulgaria's National History Museum in Sofia, by an anonymous 87-year-old donor. Etruscans were an ancient race of people that migrated from Lydia – in now what would be modern Turkey – settling in central Italy nearly 3 thousand years ago.

478. The Gram Code of African Adam: 450,000 Years of Africa's Lost Civilizations (Book One on Acholonu's African Adam Trilogy), Revised Edition with Ajay Prabhakar. (Catherine Acholonu's Adam Trilogy, Vol 1 in the African Adam Series):by Catherine Acholonu and Dr. Ajay Prabhakar

479. The Archaeology of Ancient Egypt: Beyond Pharaohs by Douglas J. Brewer

480. Ancient Egypt: Foundations of a Civilization: by Douglas J. Brewer

481. Egypt's Legacy: The Archetypes of Western Civilization: 3000 to 30 BC: by Michael Rice

482. What Really Happened in Ancient Times: A Collection of Historical Biographies: by Terri Johnson, Jennaya Dunlap, et al.

483. Egypt and the Egyptians, Second Edition: by Douglas J. Brewer

484. [Dogs in Antiquity: Anubis to Cerberus: Anubis to Cerberus - The Origins of the Domestic Dog (Aris and Phillips Classical Texts)] [Author: Brewer, Douglas J.] [February, 2002]:by Douglas J. Brewer

485. Who's Who in Ancient Egypt: by Michael Rice

486. Fish and Fishing in Ancient Egypt (The Natural History of Egypt):by Douglas J. Brewer

487. Egypt's Making: The Origins of Ancient Egypt 5000-2000 BC by Michael Rice (2003-12-20):by Michael Rice;

488. Things Fall Apart: Chinua Achebe

489. Grand Unified Theorem: Representation of the Unified Field Theory or the Theory of Everything: by Gabriel A. Oyibo

490. **Grand Unified Theorem: Discovery of the Theory of Everything and the Fundamental Building Block of Quantum Theory: by Gabriel A. Oyibo**

491. **Highlights of the Grand Unified Theorem: Formulation of the Unified Field Theory or the Theory of Everything:** by Gabriel A. Oyibo

492. **Egypt: The World of the Pharaohs: by Regine Schulz and Matthias Seidel**

493. **The Wisdom of Ancient Egypt by Joseph Kaster (1995-11-10):by Joseph Kaster**

494. **They Lived Before Adam ((Prehistoric Origins of the Igbo The Never Been Ruled)) by Catherine Acholonu, Dr. Ajay Prabhakar, et al.**

495. **The Invention of the Jewish People: by Shlomo Sand and Yael Lotan**

496. **The Thirteenth Tribe the Khazar Empire and Its Heritage: By Arthur Koestler and Sam Sloan**

497. **The Ten Tribes of Israel: Or the True History of the North American Indians: by Timothy R. Jenkins**

498. The Ten Tribes of Israel: Or the True History of the North American Indians: by Timothy R. Jenkins

499. The Ancient Egyptians For Dummies: by Charlotte Booth

500. Exploring The Great Pyramid of Giza: One of the Seven Wonders of the World - History Kids Books | Children's Ancient History: by Baby Professor (for kids)

501. The Old, Middle and New Kingdoms of Ancient Egypt - Ancient History 4th Grade | Children's Ancient History: by Baby Professor

502. Men and Women Were Equals in Ancient Egypt! History Books Best Sellers | Children's Ancient History: by Baby Professor

Emily Teeter

503. Religion and Ritual in Ancient Egypt Jun 13, 2011:by Emily Teeter

504. Picturing the Past: Imaging and Imagining the Ancient Middle East (Oriental Institute Museum Publications):by Jack Green, Emily Teeter, et al.

505. Scarabs, Scaraboids, Seals and Seal Impressions from Medinet Habu (Oriental Institute Publications) by Emily Teeter (2003-08-15) by Emily Teeter; Terry G. Wilfong

Contacts

Email address-lmdumizulu@gmail.com

gopegresources@gmail.com

website: https://www.maarifado.com

.

22858316R00046